EPIC BOOKS are no ordinary books. They burst with intense action, high-speed heroics, and shadows of the unknown. Are you ready for an Epic adventure?

This edition first published in 2023 by Bellwether Media, Inc.

No part of this publication may be reproduced in whole or in part without written permission of the publisher. For information regarding permission, write to Bellwether Media, Inc., Attention: Permissions Department, 6012 Blue Circle Drive, Minnetonka, MN 55343.

Library of Congress Cataloging-in-Publication Data

LC record for Porsche 718 Cayman GT4 available at: https://lccn.loc.gov/2022044147

Text copyright © 2023 by Bellwether Media, Inc. EPIC and associated logos are trademarks and/or registered trademarks of Bellwether Media, Inc.

Editor: Rachael Barnes   Designer: Jeffrey Kollock

Printed in the United States of America, North Mankato, MN

TABLE OF CONTENTS

ROARING BY	4
ALL ABOUT THE 718 CAYMAN GT4	6
PARTS OF THE 718 CAYMAN GT4	12
THE 718 CAYMAN GT4'S FUTURE	20
GLOSSARY	22
TO LEARN MORE	23
INDEX	24

ROARING BY »

The driver turns the key. The engine roars.
The Porsche 718 Cayman GT4 takes off!

4

ALL ABOUT THE 718 CAYMAN GT4

PORSCHE FACTORY IN STUTTGART, GERMANY

Porsche began making cars in 1948 in Stuttgart, Germany. The company's sports cars and engines are still made there today.

Porsche produces cars for the road and the racetrack. The 911 and Boxster are famous **models**.

1978 PORSCHE 911 SC

📍 WHERE IS IT MADE?

EUROPE

STUTTGART, GERMANY

The first Porsche Cayman was sold in 2006. The "718" was added to the Cayman name in 2016. The historic number was used on Porsche race cars in the 1950s and 1960s.

2006 CAYMAN

718 CAYMAN GT4 BASICS

YEAR FIRST MADE — 2016

COST — starts at $106,500

HOW MANY MADE — unknown

FEATURES

boxer engine

large wing

tailpipes

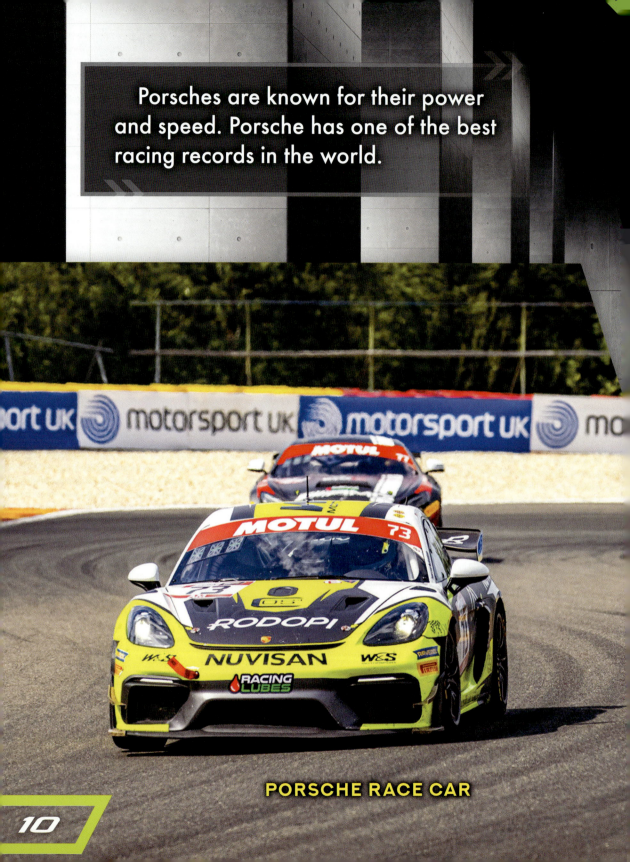

Porsches are known for their power and speed. Porsche has one of the best racing records in the world.

PORSCHE RACE CAR

CHOMP!
The Porsche Cayman is named after an animal! The caiman is a type of alligator.

2022 CAYMAN

The latest Cayman model can reach 60 miles (97 kilometers) per hour in just 4.2 seconds!

PARTS OF THE 718 CAYMAN GT4

The 718 Cayman GT4 uses a six-cylinder **boxer engine**. It is paired with a six-speed **manual transmission**. This car is known for its **handling**. The driver has control around twists and turns.

 ENGINE SPECS

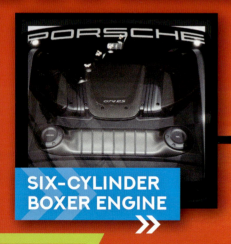

SIX-CYLINDER BOXER ENGINE

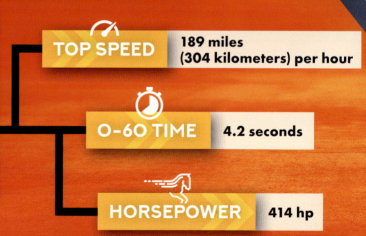

TOP SPEED — 189 miles (304 kilometers) per hour

0-60 TIME — 4.2 seconds

HORSEPOWER — 414 hp

The 718 Cayman GT4 is **aerodynamic**. A large **wing** directs air over the back of the car. It helps the car go faster!

WING

SIZE CHART

WIDTH 78.5 inches (199.4 centimeters)

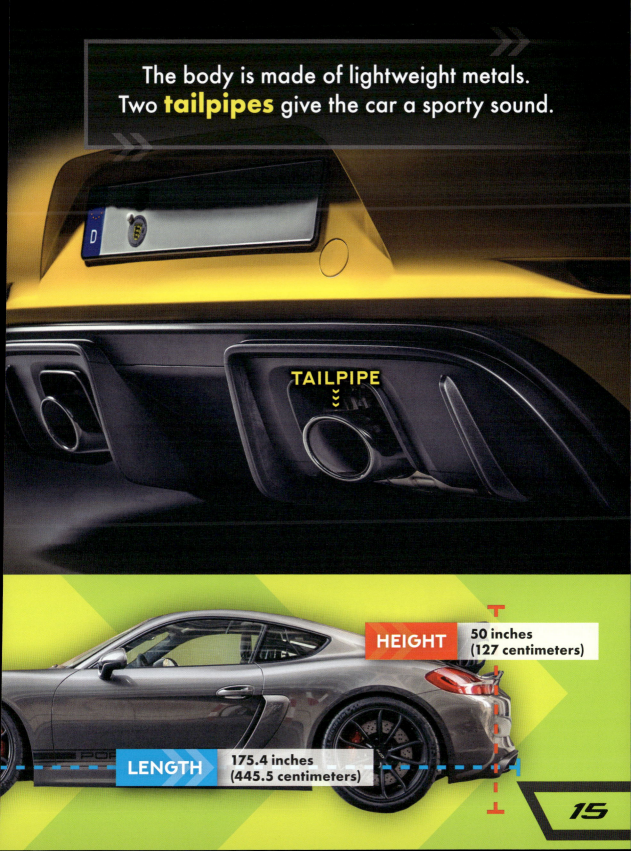

The body is made of lightweight metals. Two **tailpipes** give the car a sporty sound.

TAILPIPE

HEIGHT 50 inches (127 centimeters)

LENGTH 175.4 inches (445.5 centimeters)

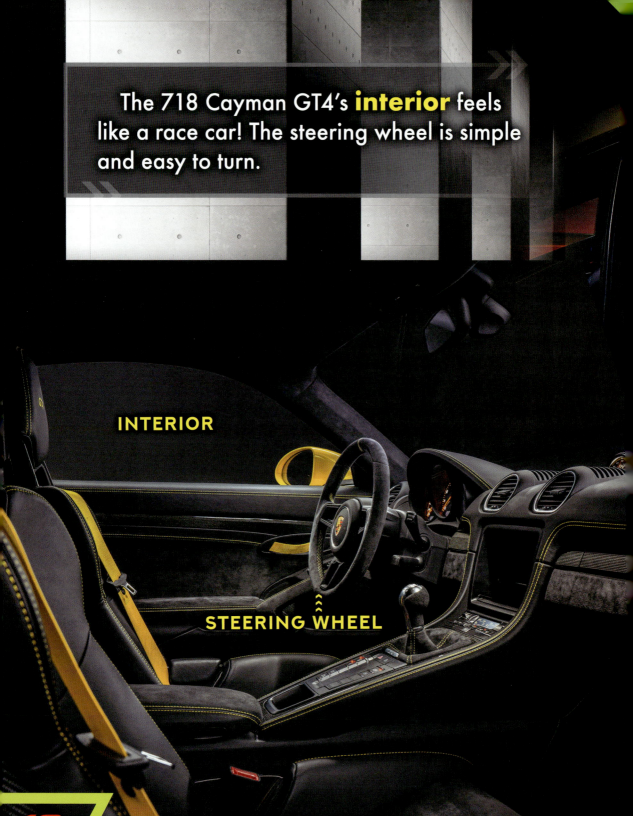

The 718 Cayman GT4's **interior** feels like a race car! The steering wheel is simple and easy to turn.

INTERIOR

STEERING WHEEL

KEEPING TIME
The 718 Cayman GT4 has a lap stopwatch. Drivers can record and save their lap times.

FABRIC HANDLE

The door handles are **fabric**.
The seatbelts come in many bright colors.

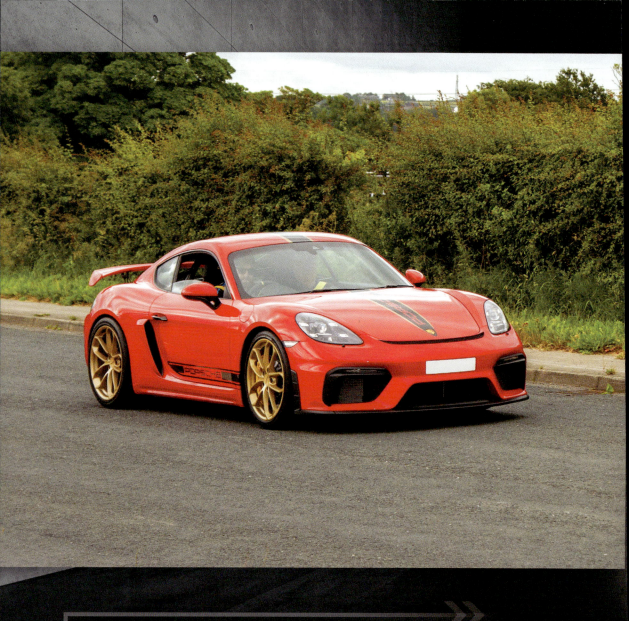

The 718 Cayman GT4 has a feature called launch control. It makes the car quickly speed up.

Porsche released a new model in 2022. The 718 Cayman GT4 RS is speedier and more powerful.

718 CAYMAN GT4 RS

THE 718 CAYMAN GT4'S FUTURE

Porsche is testing cars that do not use gasoline. By 2030, most of their cars will be **electric**.

The 718 Cayman GT4 will soon be safer for the planet!

CAR CONNECT

Drivers can control the 718 Cayman GT4 from their phones! They can lock their doors, check mileage, and find their car.

GLOSSARY

aerodynamic—able to move through air easily

boxer engine—a flat engine that has horizontal cylinders; cylinders are parts in a car's engine that take gasoline and turn it into power.

electric—able to run without gasoline

fabric—cloth or similar material made of fibers

handling—how a car performs around turns

interior—the inside of a car

manual transmission—a system that a driver uses to shift gears

models—specific kinds of cars

tailpipes—pipes used to direct gases out of a car's engine and away from the car

wing—a part on a car's body that helps it smoothly travel through air

TO LEARN MORE

AT THE LIBRARY

Adamson, Thomas K. *Porsche Taycan*. Minneapolis, Minn.: Bellwether Media, 2023.

Kingston, Seth. *The History of Porsches*. New York, N.Y.: Rosen Publishing, 2019.

Mattern, Joanne. *Porsche GT3*. Minneapolis, Minn.: Kaleidoscope, 2022.

ON THE WEB

FACTSURFER

Factsurfer.com gives you a safe, fun way to find more information.

1. Go to www.factsurfer.com.

2. Enter "Porsche 718 Cayman GT4" into the search box and click 🔍.

3. Select your book cover to see a list of related content.

INDEX

aerodynamic, 14
basics, 9
body, 15
door handles, 17
electric, 20
engine, 4, 6, 12
engine specs, 12
future, 20
handling, 12
history, 6, 8, 19
interior, 16, 17
lap stopwatch, 17
launch control, 18
manual transmission, 12
models, 7, 11, 19
name, 8, 11
phones, 21
Porsche, 6, 7, 10, 19, 20
racing, 7, 8, 10, 16

seatbelts, 17
size, 14–15
sound, 5, 15
speed, 10, 11, 14, 18, 19
steering wheel, 16
Stuttgart, Germany, 6, 7
style, 5
tailpipes, 15
wing, 14

The images in this book are reproduced through the courtesy of: VanderWolf Images, front cover, p. 9 (isolated car); Sport car hub, p. 3; Daniliuc Victor, pp. 4, 14 (wing); Jarlat Maletych, p. 5; Markus Mainka, p. 6; FernandoV, p. 7; culture-images GmbH/ Alamy, pp. 8-9; Bloomberg/ Getty Images, pp. 9 (engine), 12 (engine); classic topcar, pp. 9 (wing), 15, 16, 17; Grzegorz Czapski, p. 9 (tailpipes); DPPI Media/ Alamy, p. 10; betto rodrigues, p. 11; dimcars, p. 13; Dmitry Eagle Orlov, p. 14 (width); Tim Wilkens, p. 15 (length); Blackball Media/ Alamy, p. 17 (fabric handle); ZarkePix/ Alamy, p. 18; Brianna Leipert, p. 19; BoJack, p. 20; Colin Van Dervort/ Flickr, p. 21.